DATE DUE			

LEO MARX
THE AMERICAN REVOLUTION AND THE AMERICAN LANDSCAPE

Distinguished Lecture Series
on
the Bicentennial

revolution · continuity · promise

LEO MARX

THE AMERICAN REVOLUTION
AND THE AMERICAN LANDSCAPE

Delivered in
Cabell Hall, The University of Virginia
Charlottesville, Virginia
on March 27, 1974

American Enterprise Institute for Public Policy Research
Washington, D. C.

Although the subject I have been invited to discuss is unusual, it may not strike you as wholly unfamiliar. I say it is unusual because we do not ordinarily think of landscape as having political consequences. A landscape, after all, is an image of topography. Does it make any sense to attribute revolutionary force to a topographical image? How would the image acquire such force? To my knowledge, no political philosopher ever has addressed himself to these questions.

But though the subject of this lecture seems unusual when considered in the abstract, the specific title—"The American Revolution and the American Landscape"—sounds familiar. If anything it has a conventional schoolroom air about it, like an idea of revolution that we learned in the first grade along with the words to "America the Beautiful." The oddity of the concept of a revolutionary landscape seems to fade when we specify the *American* Revolution and the *American* landscape. To indicate what I mean, let us suppose for a moment that we are not now assembled in Charlottesville, Virginia, on a university campus designed by Mr. Jefferson, but in Paris, in a setting designed, say, for Louis XIV; and let us suppose that the revolution we are preparing to celebrate is not the one that began on the village green of Lexington in April 1775, but rather the one that began at the Bastille in July 1789. Is it conceivable that we would have gathered to discuss "The French Revolution and the French Landscape"? I think not.

The point is that our subject is not only peculiar but, as we used to say with more pride than we can muster nowadays, peculiarly American. This is not to deny that the French mind, like that of any self-conscious people, has in a degree been shaped by the place it inhabits. As Americans, however, we seem to be particularly receptive to the idea that the native landscape has had a specially important part in the formation of our national identity. The reason is obvious. From the time they first saw the New World, Europeans conceived of it symbolically, as a possible setting for a new beginning. "All these islands are very beautiful," said Columbus, describing his first landfall,

> and distinguished by a diversity of scenery; they are filled
> with a great variety of trees of immense height . . . there
> are mountains of very great size and beauty, vast plains,
> groves, and very fruitful fields, admirably adapted for
> tillage, pasture and habitation. The convenience and
> excellence of the harbours in this island, and the abun-
> dance of the rivers, so indispensable to the health of man,
> surpass anything that would be believed by one who had
> not seen it.[1]

Even here, in this letter dated March 14, 1493, the landscape has begun to work its characteristic influence upon the imagination. Of course we know that Europeans long had cherished the fantasy of disengagement from a constricted world, and a chance to begin life anew in an unspoiled landscape. It is true that the tacit invitation that we hear in Columbus's letter—the invitation to come away and enjoy a better life—is like the invitation that had been given expression in Europe's pastoral literature since Theocritus and Virgil. But the difference in this instance is important too. This time the place to which we are being invited is not an imaginary Arcadia, but a real land with real pastures and real trees. More than any other quality, then, it is the unique tangibility of this ideal landscape, so unspoiled, so rich, so beautiful—in a word, so inviting—that accounts for its exceptionally powerful hold upon the imagination. The power of this imagery is reflected in the work of our classic American writers (Cooper, Emerson,

---

[1] Christopher Columbus, *Four Voyages to the New World,* ed., R. H. Major (New York: Corinth Books, 1961) , pp. 5-6.

Thoreau, Hawthorne, Melville, Whitman, Mark Twain, Frost, Faulkner, Hemingway), where the landscape is no mere setting or backdrop, but an active shaping force in the consciousness of men and women. If our imaginative writers are correct, the landscape may be a decisive clue to the understanding of American thought and behavior. Let me illustrate with a familiar example, F. Scott Fitzgerald's *The Great Gatsby,* which happens to be enjoying a conspicuous vogue right now. Today we tend to read *Gatsby* as a tragic fable written in the peculiar hybrid mode of pastoral-romance developed by American writers. But it also can be read as a kind of mystery story. I want to call attention to the mystery, which inheres (as it turns out) in the national character itself, and to the remarkable device that Fitzgerald uses, finally, to dispel the mystery.

Gatsby's story is told, you will recall, by Nick Carraway, a young man from Minnesota who comes East in the spring of 1922 to make his fortune in Wall Street. The novel turns on Nick's effort to understand the behavior of his legendary, mysterious neighbor—the former James Gatz of North Dakota. To Nick, Gatsby represents, as he says, "everything for which I have un-affected scorn." What he scorns is Gatsby's vulgar display of wealth (exemplified by his ostentatious parties and his burnished, cream-colored car), not to mention his ruthless and even criminal methods of making money. And yet Nick cannot help admiring the man. Above all, he admires Gatsby's single-minded devotion to one ideal, his absolute commitment to winning back Daisy, his first love. It is the man's "extraordinary gift for hope," his belief in the possibility of erasing the past (the five years since his rhapsodic affair with Daisy), that leads Nick to tell Gatsby, "You're worth the whole damn bunch put together." But until the very end Nick is unable to make up his mind about the man. He cannot fathom the strange blend of moral obtuseness and idealism in Gatsby, and so throughout his telling of the story he wavers between scorn and admiration. It is only when the summer is over, after Gatsby has been murdered, that Nick finally discovers the missing clue. Just before going back to Minnesota, his trunk packed, he returns to the shore near Gatsby's house for a final look. It is evening, and in the moonlight he sees the landscape as he imagines it once had appeared to arriving Europeans. Only

3

then does he recognize the origin of Gatsby's contradictory and self-destructive behavior.

> Most of the big shore places were closed now and there were hardly any lights except the shadowy, moving glow of a ferryboat across the Sound. And as the moon rose higher the inessential houses began to melt away until gradually I became aware of the old island here that flowered once for Dutch sailor's eyes—a fresh, green breast of the new world. Its vanished trees, the trees that had made way for Gatsby's house, had once pandered in whispers to the last and greatest of all human dreams; for a transitory enchanted moment man must have held his breath in the presence of this continent, compelled into an aesthetic contemplation he neither understood nor desired, face to face for the last time in history with something commensurate to his capacity for wonder.[2]

What this extraordinarily resonant passage implies is nothing less than an explanation of the formation of the American character and, by extension, of our national behavior. It says that what happened to Gatsby, both how he came to be the man he was and how he brought on his own defeat, can only be understood in the light of the special way that Europeans perceived the New World. The sight of an unspoiled, unstoried green continent nurtured certain propensities of thought and action which are still operative five centuries after Columbus's first landfall. It is important to notice, also, that Nick describes that flowering landscape, back of the momentarily vanished houses, as having "pandered" to the dreams of his prototypical American. With that one devastating word, Fitzgerald quietly insinuates a dark view of the effect of the landscape upon the native consciousness. I will return to that theme. Here it is only necessary to emphasize the importance of this retrospective image of the unspoiled American continent. Without it, Fitzgerald tells us, Nick could not have penetrated the mystery of Gatsby and his ambiguous greatness. I do not know any work of literature that invests

---

[2] *The Great Gatsby* (New York: Charles Scribner's Sons, 1953), pp. 2, 154, 182.

an image of landscape with greater significance, and in fact, it is difficult to imagine how it could.

But there also is something anomalous about the notion that Americans are, or have been, uniquely responsive to their natural surroundings. Compared with other peoples, surely, we have not been distinguished for cherishing the environment. If there is anything distinctive about the American experience of the land, it is the brevity of our tenure and the fact that we often made the land a commodity before using it as a habitation. "The land was ours," in Robert Frost's words, "before we were the land's."[3] So, far from having a particularly enduring and affectionate attachment to the places we inhabit, Americans probably are the least rooted, the most casually nomadic of modern peoples. Moreover, the nation's record as a user of forests, grasslands, wildlife, and water sources has been, in the judgment of one knowledgeable observer, "the most violent and the most destructive of any written in the long history of civilization."[4]

No, the unique significance of the landscape in the American consciousness is not to be confused with reverence for the land as such. Rather, as Fitzgerald understood, its significance is chiefly symbolic. It is a central feature of our myth of national origins. According to that myth, it is the landscape that initially invited Europeans to disengage themselves from a constricted social environment and to begin a simpler, freer, more fulfilling life in the unstoried terrain of North America. When Nick gazes at the shore in the moonlight, when he summons an image of the way it looked to the first Europeans, he suddenly recognizes the source of Gatsby's "heightened sensitivity to the promises of life." Once the landscape had been the embodiment of those promises. Like Columbus or the Dutch sailors or the millions who followed them, Gatsby had believed that tomorrow, any tomorrow, he could have erased the past and begun a new life—the sort of life that only exceptional beauty, wealth, and freedom make possible. If Americans have a peculiar inclination to experience the world in this way, it is because the idea of a new beginning once had, or at

---

[3] "The Gift Outright," *Complete Poems of Robert Frost* (New York: Henry Holt and Co., 1959), p. 467.
[4] Fairfield Osborn, *Our Plundered Planet* (New York: Little Brown & Co., Inc., 1948), p. 175.

least seemed to have had, a credible basis in topographical fact. That unspoiled continent once had been there, a tangible landscape of limitless possibilities, and it informed everything that Europeans did when they came to America.

And this brings me back to our subject, for in politics the only action that can be described as a genuine new beginning is a revolution. It is fitting, therefore, that the first successful large-scale modern revolution—"successful" in the sense that it led to the establishment of a wholly new polity—was enacted by Americans. I want to suggest some of the ways in which the topographical image of a fresh start lent an impetus to the revolutionary spirit, and how it may help to account for the unusual character of the American Revolution, as well as for our subsequent failure to abide by its principles. I shall discuss four specific attributes of the New World landscape: its significance as an image of space, of time, of wealth, and of the ultimate values presumed to be inherent in nature.

II

To Europeans the most important physical attribute of the American landscape no doubt was space itself—real, open, seemingly boundless and unclaimed space. It is worth recalling that modern Europeans first began to take an interest in landscape as an aesthetic subject, exemplified by the painting of landscape for its own sake, during the age of exploration.[5] Before that time European art and literature seems to reflect a sense of being hemmed in—of being confined to old, used, closed spaces. When the idealizing imagination of Europeans had taken flight, it had tended to move in time rather than space. Such dreams of felicity as we identify with the Golden Age or with Eden or Arcadia draw most of their vitality from their location in time. It is their temporal distance, their "pastness," rather than a particular topography, that invests these ideal worlds with most of their power. A similar point can be made about the

---

[5] Kenneth Clark, *Landscape into Art* (Edinburgh: Penguin Books, 1956).

future-oriented utopias of the Renaissance. But the availability of space outside of Europe, and particularly in the hospitable climate of North America, changed all that. Here was usable space that enabled Europeans to act out that most ancient primordial urge to get away, to take a trip, to begin life again in an unspoiled landscape.

Of the many versions of the redemptive journey into the wilderness known to the revolutionary generation of Americans, perhaps the most vivid was the migration of the people of Israel, or its individual counterpart, the retreat of the Old Testament prophet into the desert. Such withdrawals from the world into nature made possible a spiritual redemption, a new sense of righteous purpose and commitment, a zeal for the triumph of justice like that of the American patriots. Thus John Adams explains the inspiriting force of the analogy in a letter to his wife, Abigail, dated June 11, 1775. He is in Philadelphia as a delegate to the Second Continental Congress, and he has just come from hearing a Mr. Duffield preach. "His discourse," writes Adams, "was a kind of exposition on the thirty-fifth chapter of Isaiah. America was the wilderness and the solitary place, and he said it would be glad, 'rejoice and blossom as the rose.' " Adams then paraphrases the sermon on points of similarity between the prophecies of Isaiah and the prospects of the embattled Americans: " 'No lion shall be there, nor any ravenous beast shall go up thereon, but the redeemed shall walk there.' " In essence the analogy is topographical. It works only so far as the colonists are prepared to see themselves, like the Hebrew prophet, as having been redeemed by their journey into desert places. (The "deserts of North America" was a stock phrase of the period.) In his letter Adams testifies to the emotional power of the metaphor. The preacher, he says, "applied the whole prophecy to this country, and gave us as animating an entertainment as I ever heard. He filled and swelled the bosom of every hearer." [6] From the viewpoint of an Adams, of course, the application was bound to be effective. It comported with the New Englander's millennial conception of

[6] *Familiar Letters of John Adams and His Wife Abigail Adams, During the Revolution,* ed., Charles Francis Adams (Freeport, New York: Books For Libraries Press, 1970) , p. 65.

American history. Had not the Puritan ancestors of John Adams, as he wrote elsewhere, "resolved to fly to the wilderness for refuge from the temporal and spiritual principalities and powers, and plagues and scourges of their native country"? [7]

But the idea of the special almost sacred character of North American space did not appeal only to sons of the Puritans. When Tom Paine wrote *Common Sense,* late in 1775, he had been in the colonies for only one year. Yet that most effective of revolutionary pamphlets is steeped in a similar kind of geographical awareness. "The Reformation," Paine writes, "was preceded by the discovery of America: As if the Almighty graciously meant to open a sanctuary to the persecuted in future years, when home should afford neither friendship nor safety." In addition to the seeming emptiness of American space (hence its availability as an asylum for the oppressed), Paine emphasized the monumental dimensions of this virgin landscape. Throughout he writes as if there were some necessary affinity between great size, the sheer extent of the continental terrain, and the great merit of the American cause. "The sun never shone on a cause of greater worth. 'Tis not the affair of a city, a county, a province, or a kingdom; but of a continent—of at least one eighth part of the habitable globe." [8]

The degree to which the idea of revolution was nurtured by the topographical awareness of the colonists cannot be established with any precision. It is the kind of link between feeling and action which the actors seldom make explicit, and for evidence the historian must attend to innovations or shifts in language. When Paine relates the worth of the American cause to the fact that it is the affair, not of a mere political unit, like a city or a kingdom, but of a topographical entity—a continent—he is giving voice to a pervasive if amorphous feeling. As the revolutionary fervor of the Americans rose between 1774 and 1776, they invoked the words *continent* and *continental* more and more often. When the delegates to the first Congress assembled, in September 1774,

---

[7] "On the Feudal and the Canon Law," in Gordon S. Wood, ed., *The Rising Glory of America, 1760-1820* (New York: George Braziller, Inc., 1971), p. 28.

[8] *The Complete Writings of Thomas Paine,* ed., Philip S. Foner, 2 vols. (New York: The Citadel Press, 1945), vol. 1, pp. 21 and 17.

they did not call themselves the "Continental Congress"; but before it was over, that term, along with terms like "continental currency" and "continental army," had come into use. The identification of the revolutionary cause with the huge North American land mass was a source of courage and hope. It was obviously reassuring for John Adams to be able to write, in another letter to his wife, this curious sentence: "The continent is really in earnest, in defending the country." [9] In retrospect there is a certain pathos, along with the unmistakable brag, about the popularity of the word "continent" in 1776. One hundred and fifty years had passed since settlement began, and yet here were the spokesmen for a thin line of colonies, still largely confined to a narrow strip along the eastern seaboard, describing themselves as an entire *continent* in revolt.

It was not difficult for a brilliant polemicist like Paine to invest the American landscape with revolutionary significance. In *Common Sense* he repeatedly translates indisputable geographical facts into arguments for independence. " 'Tis repugnant to reason," he writes, "to the universal order of things, to all examples from former ages, to suppose that this continent can long remain subject to any external power. . . . Reconciliation is *now* a fallacious dream. Nature has deserted the connection, and art cannot supply her place." A large part of what Paine meant by "common sense" was a simple environmentalism, an assumption that people's interests inevitably are determined by the place they inhabit. It is folly to argue, Paine writes, that Americans should accept the royal veto merely because British subjects living in England do. Geography makes all the difference:

> England being the king's residence, and America not so,
> makes quite another case. The king's negative here is ten
> times more dangerous and fatal than it can be in England;
> for there he will scarcely refuse his consent to a bill for

---

[9] *Familiar Letters,* June 17, 1775, p. 65. No historian I have read has explained the sudden vogue of the word "continental." It may have originated in the British Parliament, when members wanted to distinguish between the West Indian island colonies, which remained loyal to the Crown, and the rebellious American colonies. It seems likely that the Americans then took up the seemingly invidious distinction as a taunt and a boast.

putting England into as strong a state of defense as possible, and in America he would never suffer such a bill to be passed.

Like Franklin, Paine loved to taunt the British with their presumptuous smallness. "There is something absurd," he writes, "in supposing a Continent to be perpetually governed by an island." Topography, after all, is a visible embodiment of those laws of nature to which the Declaration will appeal as a sanction for revolution. "In no instance," Paine wrote, "hath nature made the satellite larger than its primary planet; and as England and America, with respect to each other, reverse the common order of nature, it is evident that they belong to different systems. England to Europe; America to itself." [10]

Turning now to the second attribute of the American landscape, its seeming timelessness, I want to suggest how this also contributed to the idea of a revolutionary new beginning. But I would add that the spatial and temporal characteristics of the landscape lent credibility to the cause of revolution in opposite ways. The vast forests, mountains, rivers, prairies, and plains of North America provided tangible images of boundlessness. These physical objects served to represent ideal space. But the same virgin landscape divested time of its usual landmarks. Compared to the terrain of Britain or Western Europe, with their cities, roads, monuments and ruins, the American landscape was a blank. It was unmarked by the usual traces of history—or at least what the white men of Europe considered to be history. (The fact that the Indians seemed to lack a written record of the past was one of the many reasons that Europeans assigned them to the realm of raw nature, or "savagery," rather than to human civilization.) During the revolutionary era Americans often referred to their country as an "asylum," by which they meant a sanctuary from the forms of constraint and repression bequeathed by the past. It was a landscape that invited adjectives like "virgin" and "unstoried" and "immemorial," words that reveal how the native sense of place carried the mind beyond the usual limits of memory, tradition, and history. This unworked terrain turned thought from the past to the future. It implied that here at least the grip of the

_____
[10] Complete Writings, vol. 1, pp. 23, 26, and 24.

past upon the present was not a fixed condition of human existence, hence a fresh start was possible. By 1776 this potentially radical idea had been translated into a specific program for dissolving the political bands which connected Americans to the past. It issued in a revolutionary act of separation.

But if the unhistoried landscape reinforced the separatist or centrifugal aspect of the American Revolution, it also lent an impetus to its political corollary: the idea of founding an entirely new republic. A landscape untouched by history also could be perceived as a threatening "hideous wilderness," and it inevitably aroused fears of lawlessness. The instinctive response of many Englishmen was to go back to first principles and establish a new political order. Beginning with the Mayflower Compact, drawn up on board ship in 1620, this habit of laying political foundations by setting forth basic, higher, or fundamental law was repeated in hundreds of covenanting acts for small towns as well as religious congregations, cities and states during the colonial period. As Hannah Arendt has suggested, this penchant for the act of founding may be the feature of the American Revolution which chiefly distinguishes it from all others. She notes that not only do we call the men of our Revolution "Founding Fathers," but they thought of themselves that way.[11] In all thirteen colonies, moreover, the Declaration of Independence was accompanied by the framing of new constitutions—as if bringing to the surface a doctrine of the sovereignty of the people which had been present, in fact if not in theory, for a long while. Although seldom formulated as an abstract principle, the idea of popular sovereignty had been a practical reality at the level of local government. (In New England alone there were more than 550 organized townships by the time independence was declared.) Many historians have noted the sudden and seemingly inexplicable transformation of colonial opinion on the eve of the Revolution. After having argued exclusively for the restoration of their traditional rights as British subjects, the colonists in 1775 and 1776 abruptly adopted the radical idea of founding a new republic in which power and authority derived from the people. It is as if the idea of new beginnings, having been nurtured by the act of settling a wilderness and having

---

[11] *On Revolution* (New York: Viking Press, Inc., 1963), p. 204.

given rise to hundreds of lesser acts of founding, had by then sunk deep roots in the native consciousness.

Much of the success that we claim for the American Revolution can be attributed to the fact that it took place in an undeveloped landscape. Most revolutionary movements, no matter how much they have aspired to anti-authoritarian ideals, have had to struggle against entrenched power and authority, and in the course of the struggle they often have been compelled to recreate the kind of centralized power they initially had repudiated. But for the most part the old order against which the American revolutionists were fighting was located across the Atlantic. Besides, the very newness of the colonies tended to diminish the influence of the wealth, status, and power that some Americans had acquired by 1776. Hence the American Revolution was won without generating the degree of class hatred, fanaticism, absolutism, and violence that has often undermined revolutionary idealism. Unlike the French, Russian, or Chinese revolutionists, the Americans did not have to build their new order on the ruins of an old one. Even at the time the Americans understood why theirs had been a particularly fortunate Revolution. When a group of French officers who had fought beside the Americans were embarking for their return to Europe, a Bostonian issued this warning:

> Do not let your hopes be inflamed by our triumphs on this virgin soil. You will carry our sentiments with you, but if you try to plant them in a country that has been corrupt for centuries, you will encounter obstacles more formidable than ours. Our liberty has been won with blood; you will have to shed it in torrents before liberty can take root in the old world.[12]

The third attribute of the North American landscape that contributed to the revolutionary spirit, along with its boundlessness and timelessness, was its promise of economic fulfillment. To gaze upon these "very fruitful fields, admirably adapted for tillage, pasture and habitation," as Columbus put it in his first letter, was to imagine an escape from the chronic scarcity which Europeans had assumed to be a permanent fact of life. It is ironic to recall

---

[12] Lord Acton, *Lectures on the French Revolution* (London: Macmillan & Co., Ltd., 1925), p. 32.

that in the seventeenth and early eighteenth centuries European governments were disdainful of their North American colonies because, lacking abundant gold and silver, they were considered too poor to bother about. Whereas Central and South America were associated with fabulous wealth, North America came to be identified with a more modest comfort and economic sufficiency. By the time of the Revolution the dominant image of the American landscape was that of "improved nature," a happy middle state located between the over-civilization of the *ancien régime* and the "savagery" of the frontier. To Crèvecoeur this middle state meant a "pleasing uniformity" of economic conditions. When an Englishman first lands on the East Coast, said Crèvecoeur, he "beholds fair cities, substantial villages, extensive fields, an immense country filled with decent houses, good roads, orchards, meadows and bridges where a hundred years ago all was wild, woody, and uncultivated!" [13]

This concept of the American economy as a kind of golden mean, a perfect blend of art and nature, comported with the prevailing eighteenth-century idea of the cyclical character of social development. All civilizations were thought, like living organisms, to go through an unvarying cycle of youth, maturity, and inevitable decline. By 1750 it was widely assumed that European societies were overripe; so far as they still could generate any vitality or creativity, it would manifest itself in America. No one gave more vivid expression to this popular idea than did Bishop Berkeley in his "Verses on the Prospect of Planting Arts and Learning in America." The poem is about the emigration of the Muse, "disgusted" with the barrenness and decay of Europe, to a landscape that epitomizes freshness, youth, and hope:

> . . . happy climes, where from the genial sun
>   And virgin earth such scenes ensue,
> The force of art by nature seems outdone,
>   And fancied beauties by the true:

Here again it is the topography of North America, the "happy climes" and "virgin earth," that the poet relies upon for the credibility of his prophetic vision of "another golden age" and

---

[13] *Letters from an American Farmer*, ed., Albert E. Stone (New York: New American Library, 1963), pp. 60-61.

for the conviction with which he finally declares: "Westward the course of empire takes its way." [14]

It is difficult to exaggerate what this sense of the inevitability of American growth and development, symbolized by the beckoning landscape, meant for the morale of the revolutionary cause. By 1776 the idea of freedom from want in America was no mere promise; the colonies already had become the world's leading example of a society without poverty. In economic terms they were fulfilling precisely the ideal that was figured by the landscape of the middle state—neither too much development nor too little, neither too wealthy nor too poor. In Jefferson's language, the unique thing about America was the "lovely equality which the poor enjoy with the rich." Our term "middle class" lacks the resonance of this eighteenth-century "middle state." For the men of the Revolution it had moral, cultural, and political as well as economic implications, and they all were figured by the image of a terrain midway between a decadent Europe and a savage frontier. The republic of the middle state was to be an essentially classless— almost pastoral—society of small property holders, men who would be satisfied to fulfill the austere neoclassical ideal of economic sufficiency. This idea of the good life makes itself felt in the Declaration of Independence, and particularly in Jefferson's substitution of the "pursuit of happiness" for property in the Lockean trilogy of unalienable rights.[15] It is this moderate sensibility which distinguishes the revolutionists of 1776 from the men who made most other revolutions. No other revolution has been fought by a people in so little danger of real deprivation or so undisturbed by the guilty awareness of desperate poverty in close proximity to great wealth. Just as the American landscape represented freedom from constraint in space and in time, so it represented the scarcely credible possibility of freedom from want.

But of all the implications of the American landscape which nurtured the revolutionary spirit of a new beginning, the most

---

[14] *Berkeley's Complete Works,* ed., A. C. Fraser, 4 vols. (Oxford: Clarendon Press, 1901), vol. 4, pp. 365-366.

[15] Caroline Robbins, *The Pursuit of Happiness* (Washington, D. C.: American Enterprise Institute, 1974), and Cecelia Kenyon, "Republicanism and Radicalism in the American Revolution: An Old-Fashioned Interpretation," *William and Mary Quarterly,* third series, vol. 19, 1962, pp. 153-182.

profoundly effective (if also the most elusive) was philosophical. Here I refer to the capacity of the landscape to represent the norm of nature itself. When Europeans journeyed into the wilderness to establish new communities, they were beginning again, returning to nature, in a quite literal sense. And when, in 1776, the Congress voted to declare the independence of the colonies, they faced the issue of beginning again in an abstract, political and philosophical sense. How would they justify breaking the law and resorting to violence? This was the bedrock philosophic issue with which the Congress confronted the Committee of Five (Jefferson, Adams, Franklin, Sherman, and Livingston) when it directed them to draw up the official proclamation of independence. In effect these men were asked to provide a reasoned case on behalf of behavior which they themselves would have described, not long before, as criminal. They were asked to justify acts which they knew would be regarded by many of their contemporaries as unmitigated treason and murder. But the fact is that they had very little difficulty in marshalling their arguments. They announced to the world that they were *entitled* to make a revolution, to alter or abolish the existing government, by (in the familiar yet seldom understood phrase) "the Laws of Nature and of Nature's God."

This is not to suggest that the idea had resulted directly from their experience of the native landscape. It was ready at hand, as everyone knows, in the language of the natural rights philosophy so effectively propounded by John Locke almost a century before. To justify an unlawful seizure of power, Locke had asked Englishmen to suppose a hypothetical situation in which they found themselves living outside politically defined social space—in what he called a "state of nature." His brilliant notion was that when we imagine such a return to a presocialized setting, we will be more likely to see the purpose of government in proper perspective. We will then recognize that government is not a natural or biological necessity, like air, food, water, clothing, or shelter. Rather, men form governments for self-protection, and it follows that governments exist to serve men rather than men to serve governments. When a government ceases to provide protection, men have a right, derived from their essential being, from that initial "state of nature," to alter or abolish that government. They have a "natural right" to organize a revolution. In making this argument Locke came close to deifying the idea of nature, by which he meant a set of abstract principles or laws governing the universe and accessible to human reason. That such laws exist had been proven beyond all doubt by the astonishing discoveries of Galileo, Kepler and Newton. Although science had discovered the physical principles of natural order and harmony, their political counterparts had yet to be fully apprehended. Locke's theory of the natural right of revolution was intended to fill that gap.

But if Englishmen of the eighteenth century were responsive to the doctrine of natural rights, consider how much more it meant to their colonial relatives. For a century and a half the colonists had been accustomed to thinking of themselves as living, if not in a state of nature, at least at a considerable distance from the centers of urbane civilization. The colonists were indisputably and irrevocably provincials, and although earlier they may have been embarrassed by the idea, during the Revolution they embraced it. The pervasive environmentalism of the age enabled them to make a virtue of provinciality. For if thought and behavior is in large measure determined by the environment, and if the ultimate principles of order lie hidden behind the mask of nature, then an American obviously was far more likely to gain access to those principles than a Londoner or a Parisian. Thus the American landscape effected a virtual religious conversion. When Englishmen set foot on American soil, said Crèvecoeur, they experienced a kind of "resurrection"—they became new men. This idea accorded perfectly with the criticism of a corrupt society developed by disaffected Englishmen at home. Adapted to American needs, the fashionable neoclassic and radical Whig social criticism meant that coarse native homespun, like provincial manners, was more natural, honest, and virtuous than imported silk or London coffee house sophistication. In America, as in republican Rome, access to a "natural" rural setting was thought to be conducive to sound anti-monarchical views. At a time when Englishmen believed that the simple life, repose, and contemplation in the countryside helped to breed republican manners, the American landscape inevitably was perceived as a seedbed of republican virtue.

What I have been trying to suggest is that the topographical awareness of Americans coincided with John Locke's philosophical argument on behalf of revolution. Even in the seventeenth century Locke had had a glimpse of this truth. "In the beginning," he said, speaking of the willingness of men in a state of nature to be satisfied with the conveniences of life, "all the world was America." [16] When Englishmen migrated they in effect were approximating a return to that natural state in which men are best able to perceive self-evident truths. The Lockean doctrine of natural rights thus provided a philosophical confirmation of a viewpoint that seemed to arise, almost spontaneously, from American soil. If the four attributes of the native landscape I have been discussing have a common significance it is, most simply put, that they reinforce the idea of freedom from constraint. The apparent limitlessness of space, the seeming absence of history, the promise of abundance, the accessibility of Nature's God—all of these were made visible, tangible, literally available (or so it seemed) by the American landscape. This was the green beacon that attracted millions of English and European migrants to America. The white colonists who rebelled against Britain in 1776 constituted a self-selected population of men and women with a special responsiveness to the idea of a fresh start. With few exceptions, either they themselves, or their ancestors, had at some point chosen to leave an old and organized society and to begin a new life in the fresh green terrain of the New World.

In conclusion, let us briefly reconsider the idea of a political new beginning to which the American landscape lent so much credibility. What has happened to the native spirit of revolution since 1776? One answer to that question is implicit in F. Scott Fitzgerald's image of the continental landscape with which we began. When Nick Carraway, the narrator of *The Great Gatsby,* imagines seeing the New World as it had flowered once for Dutch sailors' eyes, he says that the landscape

[16] "An Essay Concerning . . . Civil Government," ed., E. A. Burtt, *The English Philosophers from Bacon to Mill* (New York: The Modern Library, 1939) , p. 422.

had *"pandered* in whispers to the last and greatest of all human dreams. . . ." With that one shocking verb he intimates a somber view of the eventual effect of the landscape upon the American consciousness. To pander is to minister to base passions. If the virgin land helps to explain Gatsby's "extraordinary gift for hope," it also helps to explain the corruption of that hope. In 1776, as we have seen, the landscape had reinforced an inspiriting vision of political possibilities—indeed a revolutionary commitment to a new kind of republic aimed at securing three fundamental "natural" (hence egalitarian) rights: life, liberty, and the pursuit of happiness. Today, however, it seems evident that those very attributes of the landscape which once had inspired revolutionary idealism also ministered to the passions which dissipated it.

The movement of Europeans into a wilderness perceived as boundless, empty space served as a solvent for old assumptions about the fixity of class and status. It encouraged the rebels of 1776 to dedicate themselves to the proposition, in Lincoln's words, that all men are created equal. But of course this image of an unstoried and unpeopled landscape was a distortion of reality. In it there was no place for the Indians and their culture, and the image thereby helped to justify removing them from their land, along with the trees that made way for Gatsby's palatial house. It is worth noting, incidentally, that it was protesting black Americans, spokesmen for the civil rights movement of the 1960s, who reminded us of the unmistakably (if inadvertently) ethnocentric history lesson we teach our children with that simple statement about our beginning, "Columbus discovered America"—as if the Indians had not lived here before 1492! The fact is that for all its egalitarian implications, the spatial image of America pandered to ethnocentric and potentially racist passions. If there was no place in the myth of national origins for the Indians, neither was there a place in it for America's blacks. They crossed the Atlantic not in order to be free but in order to be enslaved. In practice the more ample life for all people allegedly provided by American space has meant, above all, a more ample life for males of white British and European origin.

By the same token, the idea of escape from historical time into the immemorial North American terrain had dangerous as well as creative consequences. The image of an unstoried landscape evoked in the native consciousness a sense of unique political possibilities, but it also encouraged an excessive confidence in the ability of European colonists to throw off constraints, both external and internal, inherited from the past. In its most extravagant form the idea of a new beginning in time has proven to be as delusive as the image of limitless space. It has encouraged an excessive reliance upon strategies of disengagement as a means of solving problems. There is a telling passage in *The Great Gatsby* when Nick tries to persuade Gatsby that he cannot expect Daisy simply to erase the five years she has been married to Tom Buchanan. " 'You cannot repeat the past,' " Nick says. " 'Can't repeat the past?' he [Gatsby] cried incredulously. 'Why of course you can! . . . I'm going to fix everything just the way it was before. . . .' "[17] This habit of mind—the illusion that at any moment it is possible to erase time, to recapture a relatively ideal untainted past in order to begin again—is traceable to the myth of national origins. It accounts for the often noted American propensity for tactics of avoidance and denial. When the trees or other natural resources in a place have been used up, when a river is polluted or a city made unlivable, the instinctive native reflex has been to move out and start again somewhere else. A contemporary sociologist, Philip Slater, has called this notion that complicated problems can be flushed away the "Toilet Assumption" of American thought.[18] It is a self-deluding tendency, one that has served to deflect attention, energy, and imagination from the unavoidable problems that would have to be confronted in order to realize the aspirations of the Founding Fathers.

So, too, the promise of abundance represented by the American landscape has had the unforeseen effect of diminishing revolutionary hopes. The patriots of 1776 envisaged a nation that might make possible, for the first time in history, universal freedom from want. They hoped to achieve a relative equality of condition, a society in which none would be too rich or too poor. But the appetite for personal wealth, sharpened by the radical individualism that emerged after 1776, turned out to be more powerful

---

[17] *Gatsby*, p. 111.

[18] *The Pursuit of Loneliness: American Culture at the Breaking Point* (Boston: Beacon Press, Inc., 1970), p. 15ff.

than our egalitarian ideals. Well before the middle of the nineteenth century the acquisitive and competitive ethos of capitalism had begun to subvert the spirit of democratic revolution. While continuing to affirm the democratic principles of their Revolution, Americans in fact were reproducing a modified version of the European social structure, marked by increasingly distinct class divisions, a system of minority ownership and control of the means of production, and an uneven distribution of wealth and power. The seemingly inexhaustible riches symbolized by the landscape stimulated a passion for an endlessly rising rate of production and consumption, a goal at variance with the sober eighteenth-century ideal of economic sufficiency.

The first lecturer in this series, Professor Irving Kristol, has affirmed the compatibility of America's democratic ideals and the capitalist program of economic growth. In the opinion of the American revolutionists, he says, "poverty is abolished by economic growth, not by economic redistribution—there is never enough to redistribute." [19] Quite apart from the question of what the Founding Fathers believed—surely Jefferson cannot without qualification be included in that generalization—I would argue that it is precisely the reliance upon corporate economic growth as a means of abolishing poverty that accounts for the shameful and unnecessary persistence of poverty in the richest of industrial nations. Our vast natural wealth has ministered to those very passions the Founding Fathers had identified with a decadent European aristocracy: greed, arrogance, and the enjoyment of wasteful luxury in the presence of acute deprivation. A primary source of the disenchantment with American society that informs so much of contemporary literature is indicated by Fitzgerald's savage description of the narrow self-serving behavior of the very rich in *The Great Gatsby*. "They were careless people," Nick says of Tom and Daisy, "—they smashed up things and creatures and then retreated back into their money or their vast carelessness, or whatever it was that kept them together, and let other people clean up the mess they had made. . . ." [20]

---

[19] *The American Revolution as a Successful Revolution* (Washington, D. C.: American Enterprise Institute, 1973), pp. 13-14.

[20] *Gatsby,* pp. 180-181.

But of all the dubious passions to which the landscape pandered, perhaps the most destructive has been the national appetite for illusory notions of American virtue. It was only a short step from the exhilarating revolutionary spirit, with its justifiable sense of the republic's rare good fortune, to an exaggerated and self-righteous sense of the unique benevolence of the national character. When Europeans crossed the Atlantic, they presumably gained access to the "state of nature" itself—that is, to ultimate, sacred, redeeming values. According to the myth, the landscape of the New World was a repository of meaning formerly attributed to the deity. Freedom from the constraints of European institutions, manners, and scarcity made possible the emergence of a "new man"—an American Adam who proved to be more spontaneous, forthright, easy, good-hearted or (in a word) more natural than people elsewhere. The identification of the national character with Nature had the effect of sacralizing national aspirations. Hence any purpose adopted by Americans was likely to be perceived, like Jay Gatsby's desire to win back Daisy, "as the following of a grail." This quasi-religious belief, needless to say, no more jibed with the facts than did the belief in an escape from history into boundless space. Although the attributes of the landscape had encouraged Americans to believe in the uniqueness of their new republic, with its stirring dedication to the principle of equality, those same attributes also enabled them to recreate many of the conditions of European society which violated that principle.

IV

As we approach the bicentennial of the Revolution, we have an obligation to acknowledge the ways in which the republic of 1976 falls short of the revolutionary goals of 1776. If the green light at the end of Daisy's dock is a sadly diminished emblem of the possibilities once made available by the landscape of the New World, it also may be said to represent a diminished commitment to our own revolutionary ideals. For at least a century after 1776 the United States was the inspiration of people struggling for freedom everywhere. But today, in many parts of the world, rebels with aspirations not unlike those of the American patriots regard our government (and with good reason) as an enemy of revolutionary egalitarianism. Within the United States, moreover, attitudes toward the idea of revolution also have been changing. In recent years the word itself has regained a measure of its appeal for numbers of disaffected citizens. Once again some Americans are thinking about revolution as a conceivable recourse, a means of achieving democratic objectives, but the dismaying fact is that the revolution they contemplate would be directed against American institutions.

All of these reflections bring me back, finally, to the way Fitzgerald unlocks the mystery of Jay Gatsby's violent death. It is from the landscape that Nick learns what destroyed Gatsby. In the end he realizes that Gatsby's dream of ecstatic fulfillment, like the national vision of possibilities, also had helped to destroy the dreamer. To be sure, the myth always had fostered extravagant hopes, but in the early phase of American history, while the land was being settled, those hopes had had a far more credible basis in fact than they do in the twentieth century.

> And as I sat there [says Nick], brooding on the old unknown world, I thought of Gatsby's wonder when he first picked out the green light at the end of Daisy's dock. He had come a long way to this blue lawn, and his dream must have seemed so close that he could hardly fail to grasp it.

And just here, in the pause between sentences, Nick finally grasps the reason for Gatsby's failure. He now knows something that Gatsby had not known. "He did not know," says Nick of Gatsby, "that it [the dream] was already behind him, somewhere back in that vast obscurity beyond the city, where the dark fields of the republic rolled on under the night."

We may take this to mean that the dream of felicity figured by the American landscape, if it ever was attainable, was closer to attainment when the Republic was founded. Although the idea of America as a new beginning no longer corresponds with the facts, many Americans (like Gatsby) have continued to behave as if it did. What this means, in political terms, is that the revolutionary content of the myth has been dissipated, but the form—the habit of mind it nurtured—is with us still. In preparation for 1976, therefore, it is instructive to read *The Great Gatsby* as a cautionary fable. It helps to explain why and how we became distracted from those generous revolutionary ideals once represented by the native landscape. Perhaps that knowledge may yet encourage us to change direction and complete our uncompleted revolution.

Cover and book design: Pat Taylor

Cabell Hall,
constructed in 1895, houses the
offices and classrooms of the College of Arts and Sciences
at the University of Virginia, Charlottesville.

Pamphlets in AEI's Distinguished Lecture Series on the Bicentennial of the United States, 1973-74

- **Irving Kristol**
  The American Revolution as a Successful Revolution

- **Martin Diamond**
  The Revolution of Sober Expectations

- **Paul G. Kauper**
  The Higher Law and the Rights of Man in a Revolutionary Society

- **Robert A. Nisbet**
  The Social Impact of the Revolution

- **Gordon Stewart Wood**
  Revolution and the Political Integration of the Enslaved and Disenfranchised

- **Caroline Robbins**
  The Pursuit of Happiness

- **Peter L. Berger**
  Religion in a Revolutionary Society

- **G. Warren Nutter**
  Freedom in a Revolutionary Economy

- **Vermont Royster**
  The American Press and the Revolutionary Tradition

- **Edward C. Banfield**
  The City and the Revolutionary Tradition

- **Leo Marx**
  The American Revolution and the American Landscape

- **Ronald S. Berman**
  Intellect and Education in a Revolutionary Society

- **Kenneth B. Clark**
  The American Revolution: Democratic Politics and Popular Education

- **Seymour Martin Lipset**
  Opportunity and Welfare in the First New Nation

- **Forrest Carlisle Pogue**
  The Revolutionary Transformation of the Art of War

- **Charles Burton Marshall**
  American Foreign Policy as a Dimension of the American Revolution

  Dean Rusk
  The American Revolution and the Future

- *Now available in print at $1.00 each.*